Slow Travel

THE SMALL DELIGHTS
OF GOING AWAY

Emma Block

RP STUDIO

PHILADELPHIA

RP Studio™
Hachette Book Group
1290 Avenue of the Americas, New York, NY 10104
www.runningpress.com
@Running_Press

Printed in Singapore
First Edition: October 2021

Published by RP Studio, an imprint of Perseus Books, LLC,
a subsidiary of Hachette Book Group, Inc. The RP Studio name
and logo is a trademark of the Hachette Book Group.

The publisher is not responsible for websites (or their content)
that are not owned by the publisher.

Design by Amanda Richmond

ISBNs: 978-0-7624-9988-5

Printer COS

10 9 8 7 6 5 4 3 2 1

Welcome

I stumbled upon the idea of slow travel accidentally, when my husband and I realized that the less we did on vacation the more we enjoyed it. We love to reminisce about our past travels, and normally it's the little things that we most fondly remember—enjoying a delicious gelato in the sunshine, getting lost and stumbling onto a street lined with beautiful houses, or walking into a little local store and trying to buy a ciabatta with broken Italian and lots of hand gestures. Slow travel is about taking in your surroundings, delighting in the little things, and making lasting memories. This travel journal is full of prompts to help you observe and record those moments. Whether you're traveling to a foreign country or just exploring your own neighborhood, I hope it will help you see the world with fresh eyes.

What were your first impressions of your surroundings?

Draw or describe the view from your window.

Is your view mostly natural or man-made? Can you see far into the distance? Can you see mountains, the sea, rooftops, trees, or fields?

What colors do you most associate with where you are?

Are there any plants or flowers currently in season outside? Describe them. They could be flowers growing wild or in someone's garden, trees in bloom, or fields ready for harvest.

Make time to watch the sunrise or the sunset.

Describe it and make a note of what the time is.

Notice the color of the sky today. Is it the same shade of blue you see back home? How about the clouds? Are they fluffy or wispy? White or grey?

Look up at the sky tonight. Can you see the same constellations that you see back home?

Stand still and notice any movement happening around you. Do you see leaves rustling, traffic moving, children playing, or laundry blowing in the breeze?

What is the style of architecture around you? How would you describe it? Do buildings appear old or new, decorative or minimalist, or made of wood, brick or stone? What are the differences and similarities between the architecture here and at home?

What are you wearing today? Sketch your vacation outfit here. How do your clothes make you feel? Is your outfit different from what you usually wear at home?

When you wake up in the morning, is it different in any way to waking up at home? Do you immediately remember where you are, or does it take some time? Are you waking up earlier or later than usual? When you wake up, is the room light or dark, warm or cool?

Close your eyes and describe what can you hear right now. Think about noises close to you and noises in the distance. Are the sounds you are hearing now constant, or do they change throughout the day? Can you hear car horns beeping, cicadas chirping in the trees, people chatting over coffee, or the clanging bells of a hilltop church?

What kind of music do you hear playing? What styles are popular where you are? Think about music you might hear in a taxi, a grocery store, or a busy bar.

Go outside in the morning or evening and listen
for birds and insects. What public spaces draw the most birds?

What is the most delicious thing you've eaten recently?

Describe it. How did you discover it?

What foods are in season where you are right now?

Write a list or draw pictures of them.

Jot down your meals from the last several days.

What made them memorable?

Are there any recipes that you want to recreate when you get home? Write down the ingredients you will need.

Is there any difference in service between restaurants and cafes here and back home? Is service slow and relaxed or quick and attentive? Is there a difference in the way you ask for the check or leave a tip?

_____

_____

_____

_____

_____

_____

_____

_____

_____

_____

_____

_____

_____

_____

_____

_____

_____

_____

_____

Is there a particular local dish that you're looking
forward to eating (or already have)?

Are there any regional desserts, cakes, or cookies in the bakeries? Have you tried any?

Describe a typical local breakfast. Have you gone out for breakfast, or have you been making your own?

When do the locals eat? Is it earlier or later than back home? Do people have a mid-afternoon snack or coffee break?

Is there a culture of street food in the place you are visiting? Is food sold from carts, trucks, or market stalls?

Where do the locals shop for food? Are there open-air markets, delicatessens, or large grocery stores?

Have you tried any new drinks on vacation? Are there local brands of soda, craft beers, regional wines, or seasonal smoothies?

Where have you had the best coffee? Describe your favorite coffee shops. What beverage did you order? Is it the same thing you order at home?

Is there a specific tea culture? How do locals like to take their tea? With milk or sugar? What type of tea is most popular? Is there any ceremony around the serving of tea? Does it come in a teapot, cup, or glass?

What can you feel right now, under your fingertips or your feet?

How is the weather where you are staying? Close your eyes and concentrate on the temperature and the breeze.

Close your eyes and describe what you can smell right now.

What smells do you most associate with being on vacation? The smell of sunscreen, fragrant plants, food cooking, or the salty smell of the sea?

Have you learned any interesting facts about the area you're staying in? What is the main crop or industry of the area? When was the town or village founded? Has anyone famous ever lived in the area?

What new words or phrases have you learned?

Are you speaking a second language?

Have you made any purchases? Have you bought something for yourself or a gift for someone? Do you like to buy souvenirs?

What is one thing that you forgot to pack for your vacation? Have you replaced this item or managed without it?

Have you visited any markets? Describe what they sell and what you bought. Did you try haggling for your goods? What is your favorite market you've ever visited?

Attach any ticket stubs from your travels here.

Have you taken any forms of public transport on your vacation? Buses, trams, trains, ferries or taxis? Describe the experience.

What forms of transport seem to be most popular with local residents?

Are there any animals where you are staying?
What kinds of pets do people have with them?

What has surprised you most about the place you are visiting?

Have you had any friendly encounters on vacation?

Describe someone you talked to, and what you discussed.
Where did you meet?

Did you bring a book with you to read on vacation?

Was your choice influenced by your destination? Are you enjoying it so far? Have you had much time to read?

Have you seen any art recently? It could be street art, fine art, or folk art. Did it inspire you? Do you have a favorite art gallery?

_____

_____

_____

_____

_____

_____

_____

_____

_____

_____

_____

_____

_____

_____

_____

_____

_____

_____

_____

_____

_____

_____

_____

_____

What book would you recommend someone read before coming here?

Have you found yourself in any amusing situations while traveling? Describe what happened.

Stand outside and look straight up. What do you see?

Have you gotten lost? Describe the experience: where you were going, how you found your way, and how you felt.

_____

_____

_____

_____

_____

_____

_____

_____

_____

_____

_____

_____

_____

_____

_____

_____

_____

_____

_____

_____

_____

_____

Have you visited any areas of natural beauty, like
a city park, a beach, the woods, or the mountains?
How did spending time in nature make you feel? What is the
most beautiful place you've ever visited?

When you are outdoors, pick a couple of small flowers or leaves to press between the pages of this journal.

Make sure you only take one or two, and not from private property.

Have you developed any regular routes that you take each day? Write down the names of the roads and where they take you.

Have you taken many photos on vacation? What things have caught your eye—the landscape, famous sites, your traveling companions, your meals, or maybe yourself? Do you like to print your photos when you return home?

Have you eaten outdoors, perhaps on a restaurant patio, or at a picnic? How did being outside enhance the experience?

Do you eat or drink more indulgent meals on vacation? What foods are "vacation foods" to you?

Are the locals generally outgoing and welcoming or are they quieter and more reserved? Do people seem relaxed or busy?

What is your best memory from your trip?

Describe it as if you are telling the story to a friend.